HOW WE MAY READ THE SCRIPTURES WITH MOST SPIRITUAL PROFIT

HOW WE MAY READ THE SCRIPTURES WITH MOST SPIRITUAL PROFIT

REV. THOMAS WATSON A.M.

FORMER MINISTER AT ST. STEPHENS, WALBROOK

CURIOSMITH

MINNEAPOLIS

Published by Curiosmith.
Minneapolis, Minnesota.
Internet: curiosmith.com.

Previously published as part of *A Supplement to the Morning-Exercise at Cripple-gate: or Several More Cases of Conscience Practically Resolved by Sundry Ministers,* Samuel Annesley, edit., London: Thomas Cockerill, 1674.

The text for this edition is from: *The Morning Exercises at Cripplegate, St. Giles in the Fields and Southwark; etc.,* Vol. 2, James Nichols, edit., London: Thomas Tegg, 1844.

The notes and quotes in the footnotes are the original Greek and Latin notes translated into English by James Nichols (1785–1861).

The biography is from: Samuel Dunn. *Memoirs of the Seventy-Five Eminent Divines Whose Discourses Form the Morning Exercises Cripplegate, St. Giles in the Fields, and in Southwark.* London: John Snow, 1844.

Elizabethan verbs and pronouns are updated to modern English word for word.

The "Guide to the Contents" was added to this edition by the publisher.

ISBN 9781946145468

GUIDE TO THE CONTENTS

——∘o⟨⊚⟩oo——

Biographical Sketch of

Rev. Thomas Watson, A.M.

This pious writer and preacher received his education at Emmanuel College, Cambridge, where he was noted for being a hard student. In 1646, he became rector of St. Stephen's, Walbrook, where he faithfully and successfully discharged the duties of his office until he was ejected by the Act of Uniformity. He discovered great loyalty and attachment to Charles I, and totally disapproved of the methods used by the army to bring him to trial. In 1651, he was concerned with some others in carrying on a correspondence with the Scots, for the purpose of bringing in Charles II, which being discovered he was apprehended, and committed prisoner to the Tower.

Once on a lecture-day, the learned Bishop Richardson came to hear him, at St. Stephen's, and was so pleased with his sermon, but especially with the prayer after, that he followed him home to give him thanks, and desired a copy of it. "Alas!" said

Mr. Watson, "that is what I cannot give, for I do not use to pen my prayers; it was no studied thing, but uttered as God enabled me from the abundance of my heart." Upon this the good bishop went away astonished that any man could pray in that manner extempore.

With several other ministers, he petitioned the King against the operation of the Act of Uniformity, but without effect. August 17, he preached in the forenoon on John 13:34. He remarks,

We ought to love the saints:
1. In what condition soever they are.
2. Although they may have many infirmities.
3. Though weak in parts.
4. Though in some lesser things they differ from us.
5. When they are reviled and persecuted.
6. Though their graces may eclipse and outshine ours.

Four fruits of love to the saints:
1. We must show love to them by prizing their persons above others.
2. By vindicating them when traduced and slandered.
3. By praying for them.
4. By being ready, according to your abilities, to relieve their wants.

In the afternoon, he preached on 2 Corinthians 7:1, and on the Tuesday following on Isaiah 3:10, 11.

There is also in the volume of Farewell Sermons, one by Mr. Watson against Popery. He exhorts all Christians to flee from the following Popish errors:

1. That the pope is head of the church.
2. That the pope is above Scripture.
3. The mass, which is gross idolatry.
4. That we do in our own persons, satisfy God's justice by our penance, whipping, fasting, and alms-deeds.
5. The distinguishing between sins mortal and sins venial.
6. The doctrine of free-will; that man's will is inclinable unto good, and that a man has an *innate* power to do that which is good.
7. Indulgences.
8. The doctrine of merits.
9. Of Purgatory.
10. The invocation of angels.
11. The worshipping of images.
12. They deny that Jesus Christ suffered what was equivalent to the pains of hell.
13. They say the pope has power to absolve men from their oaths.

Besides these thirteen errors, consider these particulars:

1. The Popish religion is an impure, filthy religion, allowing of stews and brothel-houses for money.
2. It is a superstitious religion.
3. It is upheld by deceit and lying.
4. It is an outside carnal religion.

5. It is an unedifying religion, it does not build men up in their most holy faith.
6. It is a cruel religion, maintained and propagated by blood and cruelty.
7. It is a self-contradictory religion.

Therefore let me exhort you:
1. Hold fast the doctrine of the true orthodox Protestant religion.
2. Hold forth the profession of the Protestant religion.
3. Adorn the Protestant religion.

After the fire in London, in 1666, when the churches were burned, Mr. Watson and several other Nonconformists, fitted up large rooms for those who had an inclination to attend. Upon the Indulgence, in 1672, he licensed the great hall in Crosby-house, on the east side of Bishopsgate-street, then belonging to Sir John Langham, which is regarded as the most perfect specimen of domestic architecture of the fifteenth century now remaining in the metropolis. The splendid hall, which had often been the scene of high festivity and court intrigue, and had vibrated with the world's minstrelsy for more than two hundred years, thus became a place for public prayer and praise. Mr. Watson was a man of deep piety, considerable learning, a lively and judicious preacher, and eminent in the gift of prayer.

He published a variety of books, chiefly on

practical subjects. In *The Life of Colonel James Gardiner*, there is this remarkable account: "In July, 1719, he had spent the evening, which was the Sabbath, in some gay company, and had an unhappy assignation with a married lady, whom he was to attend exactly at twelve. The company broke up about eleven, and he went into his chamber to kill the tedious hour. It happened that he took up a religious book, which his good mother or aunt had, without his knowledge, slipped into his portmanteau, called *The Christian Soldier*, written by Mr. Watson. Guessing by the title that he should find some phrases of his own profession spiritualized, in a manner which might afford him some diversion, he resolved to dip into it; while this book was in his hand, an impression was made upon his mind, which drew after it a train of the most important consequences. Suddenly he thought he saw an unusual blaze of light fall on the book while he was reading, and lifting up his eyes he apprehended, to his extreme amazement, that there was before him, as it were suspended in the air, a visible representation of the Lord Jesus Christ upon the cross, surrounded with a glory; and was impressed as if a voice had come to him, to this effect: 'Oh sinner, did I suffer this for thee, and are these the returns?' He sunk down in his chair, and continued for some time insensible. He then arose in a tumult of passions, and walked to and fro in his chamber, till he was ready to drop, in unutterable astonishment and agony of heart, which continued until the October following, when his terrors were turned into unutterable joy."

Mr. Watson also published:—Discourses on the Beatitudes;—The Christian's Charter;—The Art of Divine Contentment;—The Godly Man's Picture;—A Word of Comfort;—The Doctrine of Repentance;—The Mischief of Sin;—A Divine Cordial;—The Holy Eucharist;—The Duty of Self-denial;—several sermons. After his death, there was published, his Body of Divinity, in sermons on the Assembly's Catechism. He continued his ministry in London, as he had opportunity for many years, but his strength failing, he retired into Essex, and there he died suddenly in his closet, while at prayer. His sermons in the Morning Exercises are:—How must we make religion our business?—How may we read the Scriptures with most spiritual profit?— How God is his people's great reward?—The day of judgment asserted.

HOW WE MAY READ THE SCRIPTURES WITH MOST SPIRITUAL PROFIT

by
Rev. Thomas Watson, A.M.

And it shall be with him, and he shall read therein all the days of his life: that he may learn to fear the Lord his God, to keep all the words of this law and these statutes, to do them.—DEUTERONOMY 17:19.

What Cicero said of Aristotle's Politics, may not unfitly be said of this Book of Deuteronomy: "It is full of golden eloquence." In this chapter God instructs the people of the Jews about setting a king over them. And there are two things specified in order to their king:

1. His election.
2. His religion.

1. *His election.*—"Thou shalt in any wise set him king over thee, whom the Lord thy God shall choose."[1] Good reason God should have the choice of their king, seeing "by him kings reign."[2]

1 Deuteronomy 17:15.
2 Proverbs 8:15.

2. *His religion.* "When he sitteth upon the throne of his kingdom, he shall write him a copy of this law in a book, out of that which is before the priests the Levites."[1,2] Here was a good beginning of a king's reign: the first thing he did after he sat upon the throne, was to copy out the Word of God in a book. And in the text: "It shall be with him, and he shall read therein all the days of his life: that he may learn to fear the Lord his God, to keep all the words of this law and these statutes, to do them." *It shall be with him*—The book of the law shall be his *vade mecum,* or daily companion. Charles the Great used to set his crown upon the Bible. Indeed the Bible is the best supporter of the crown. And *he shall read therein*[3]—It is not below the majesty of a prince to peruse the oracles of heaven: in them are comprised sacred apophthegms: "I will speak of excellent things."[4] In the Septuagint it is, σεμνα, "grave things;" in the Hebrew, נְגִידִים "princely things;" such as are fit for a God to speak, and a king to read. Nor must the king only read the book

---

1 Deuteronomy 17:18.

2 "The book of the law, which was of supreme authority, was carefully preserved by the Levitical priests in the inner court of the temple."—PAUL FAGIUS. *(Nichols' trans.)*

3 "It was a part of his duty to read the law, both to himself in private, and publicly in the temple, in order that the people might know that no one was exempted from its observance."—GROTIUS. *(Nichols' trans.)*

4 Proverbs 8:6.

of the law at his first installment into his kingdom, but *he shall read therein all the days of his life.—* כָּל־יְמֵי חַיָּיו He must not leave off reading till he left off reigning. And the reasons why he must be conversant in the law of God, are in the subsequent words: (1.) "That he may learn to fear the Lord his God." Reading of the Word is the best means to usher in the fear of the Lord. (2.) "That he may keep all the words of this law, to do them." (3.) "That he may prolong his days in his kingdom."

I shall now confine myself to these words: "He shall read in it," that is, the book of the law, "all the days of his life." The Holy Scripture is, as Austin says, a golden epistle sent to us from God.[1] This is to be read diligently. "Ignorance" of Scripture is "the mother of" error, not "devotion." "Ye do err, not knowing the Scriptures."[2] We are commanded to "search the Scriptures."[3] The Greek word Ερευνατε signifies to search as for a vein of silver. How diligently does a child read over his father's will and testament, and a citizen peruse his charter! With the like diligence should we read God's Word, which is our Magna Charta for heaven.[4] It is a mercy the

---

1 "What is Holy Scripture but a sort of epistle from Almighty God to his creatures, in which the words of God are heard, and by which they learn his mind?"—AUGUSTINE, in *Psalms.* (*Nichols' trans.*)

2 Matthew 22:29.

3 John 5:39.

4 "The Bible invites an attentive reader, but rejects one who

Bible is not prohibited. Trajan the emperor for-
bade the Jews to read in the book of the law. Let us
inquire at this sacred oracle. Apollos was "mighty in
the Scriptures."[1] Melancthon, when he was young,
sucked αδολον γαλα, "the sincere milk of the Word."[2]
Alphonsus, king of Arragon, read over the Bible four-
teen times. That Roman lady Cecilia had, by much
reading of the Word, made her breast *bibliothecam
Christi*, "the library of Christ," as Jerome speaks.[3]
Were the Scriptures only in their original tongue,
many would plead excuse for not reading; but when
"this sword of the Spirit" is unsheathed, and the Word
is made plain to us by being translated, what should
hinder us from a diligent search into these holy mys-
teries? Adam was forbid, upon pain of death, to taste
of the tree of knowledge: "In the day that thou eatest
thereof thou shalt surely die."[4] But there is no dan-
ger of touching this tree of Holy Scriptures; if we
do *not* eat of this tree of knowledge, we shall surely
die. What will become of them who are strangers to
Scripture? "I have written to him the great things of

---

is slothful."—RIVET *Isagoge ad Scripturas.* (*Nichols' trans.*)

1 Acts 18:24.

2 MELCHIOR ADAMUS *in Vitâ Melancthonis.*

3 "If Alexander valued Homer so highly, and Scipio Africanus
scarcely ever allowed the Cyropaedia of Xenophon to be out
of his hands, how ought we to act with regard to the sacred
volume?"—QUISTORPIUS. *See* CHYTRAEI *Praelect. in Jos., et*
MORNAEUM. (*Nichols' trans.*)

4 Genesis 2:17.

my law; but they were counted as a strange thing."[1]
Many lay aside Scripture as rusty armor;[2] they are
better read in romances than in St. Paul; they spend
many hours *inter pectinem et speculum,* "between the
comb and the glass;" but their eyes begin to be sore
when they look upon a Bible. The very Turks will
rise up in judgment against these Christians: they
reverence the books of Moses; and if they find but
a leaf wherein any thing of the Pentateuch is written, they take it up and kiss it. They who slight the
Word written, slight God himself, whose stamp it
bears. To slight the king's edict, is an affront offered
to the person of the king. Scripture-vilifiers are in a
damnable state.[3] "Whoso despiseth the Word shall
be destroyed."[4] Nor is it enough to read the Word
of God, but it should be our care to get some spiritual emolument and profit by it, that our souls may
be εντρεφομενοι, "nourished up in the words of
faith."[5] Why else was the Scripture written, but that
it might profit us? God did not give us his Word
only as a landscape, to look upon; but he delivered it
to us, as a father delivers a stock of money to his son,
to improve. It is sad not to profit by the Word, to be
like a body in an atrophy, that does not thrive: men

---

1 Hosea 8:12.
2 Jeremiah 8:9.
3 "Those who reject the oracles of God, entangle themselves
in intricate and destructive snares."—CALVIN. *(Nichols' trans.)*
4 Proverbs 13:13.
5 1 Timothy 4:6.

would be loath to trade, and get no profit.

QUESTION. The grand question I am to speak to is this: *How we may read the Scriptures with most spiritual profit.* It is a momentous question, and of daily use.

RESPONSE. For the resolution of this question, I shall lay down several rules or directions about reading of Scripture.

DIRECTION 1. *If you would profit by reading, remove those things which will hinder your profiting.*—That the body may thrive, obstructions must be removed. There are three obstructions [that] must be removed, if you would profit by Scripture.

1. *Remove the love of every sin.*[1]—Let a physician prescribe never so good receipts, if the patient takes poison, it will hinder the virtue and operation of the physic. The Scripture prescribes excellent receipts; but sin lived-in poisons all. The body cannot thrive in a fever; nor can the soul, under the feverish heat of lust. Plato calls the love of sin *magnus daemon*, "a great devil." As the rose is destroyed by the canker which breeds in it, so are the souls of men by those sins they live in.

2. *Take heed of the thorns which will choke the Word read.*—These thorns our Saviour expounds to be "the cares of this world."[2] By "cares" is meant

---

1 "Most persons slightly graze their sins, but do not totally eradicate them."—BERNARD. *(Nichols' trans.)*
2 Matthew 8:22.

covetousness.[1] A covetous man is a pluralist; he has such diversity of secular employments, that he can scarce find time to read; or if he does, what solecisms does he commit in reading! While his eye is upon the Bible, his heart is upon the world; it is not the writings of the apostles he is so much taken with, as the writings in his account-book. Is this man likely to profit? You may as soon extract oils and syrups out of a flint, as he any real benefit out of Scripture.

3. *Take heed of jesting with Scripture.*—This is playing with fire. Some cannot be merry unless they make bold with God. When they are sad, they bring forth the Scripture as their harp to drive away the evil spirit.[2] As that drunkard who, having drunk off his cups, called to his fellows, "Give us of your oil, for our lamps are gone out." In the fear of God beware of this.[3] King Edward IV would not endure to have his crown jested with, but caused *him* to be executed *who* said he would make his son heir to the crown,[4] meaning the sign of the crown: much less will God endure to have his Word jested with. Eusebius relates of one who took a piece of Scripture to jest with, [that] God struck him with frenzy. The Lord may

1 "Money is the sole object of their gaze and pursuit."—NICHOLS.
2 "Fly, ye profane! far, far away remove."—VIRGIL *Aeneid.* book 6. 258; *(Pitt's trans.)*
3 "Those whom it is the will of God to destroy, he permits to jest and trifle with the Holy Scripture."—LUTHER. *(Nichols' trans.)*
4 SPEED's Chronicle.

justly give over such persons, εις αδοκιμον νουν, "to a reprobate mind."[1]

DIRECTION 2. *If you would profit, prepare your hearts to the reading of the Word.*—The heart is an instrument [that] needs putting in tune. "Prepare your hearts unto the Lord."[2] The Heathens (as Plutarch notes) thought it indecent to be too hasty or rash in the service of their supposed deities.[3] This preparation to reading consists in two things: (1.) *In summoning our thoughts together to attend that solemn work we are going about.*—The thoughts are stragglers; therefore rally them together. (2.) *In purging out those unclean affections which do indispose us to reading.*—The serpent, before he drinks, casts up his poison. In this we should be "wise as serpents;" before we come to these "waters of life," [we should] cast away the poison of impure affections. Many come rashly to the reading of the Word; and no wonder, if they come without preparation, [that] they go away without profit.

DIRECTION 3. *Read the Scripture with reverence.* —Think every line you read God is speaking to you. The ark, wherein the law was put, was overlaid with pure gold, and was carried on bars, that the Levites might not touch it.[4] Why was this, but to breed in the

---

1 Romans 1:28.

2 1 Samuel 7:3.

3 "They do not worship in a cursory manner."—PLUTARCH. *(Nichols' trans.)*

4 Exodus 25:10–15.

people reverence to the law? When Ehud told Eglon he had a message to him from God, he arose from his throne.[1] The Word written is a message to us from Jehovah; with what veneration should we receive it!

DIRECTION 4. *Read the books of Scripture in order.*—Though occurrences may sometimes divert our method, yet for a constant course it is best to observe an order in reading. Order is an help to memory: we do not begin to read a friend's letter in the middle.

DIRECTION 5. *Get a right understanding of Scripture.*—"Give me understanding, that I may learn thy commandments."[2] Though there are some, δυσνοητα, knots in Scripture, which are not easily untied; yet things essential to salvation the Holy Ghost has plainly pointed out to us. The knowledge of the sense of Scripture is the first step to profiting. In the law Aaron was first to light the lamps, and then to burn the incense: the lamp of the understanding must be first lighted, before the affections can be inflamed. Get what knowledge you can by comparing Scriptures, by conferring with others, by using the best annotators. Without knowledge, the Scripture is a sealed book; every line is too high for us; and if the Word shoot above our head, it can never hit our heart.

DIRECTION 6. *Read   the   Word   with*

1 Judges 3:20.
2 Psalm 119:73.

seriousness.—"If one go over the Scripture curso-rily," says Erasmus, "there is little good to be got by it; but if he be serious in reading of it, it is the 'savor of life.'" And well may we be serious, if we consider the importance of those truths which are bound up in this sacred volume. "It is not a vain thing for you;[1] because it is your life."[2] If a letter were to be broken open and read, wherein a man's whole estate were concerned, how serious would he be in reading of it! In the Scripture our salvation is concerned; it treats of the love of Christ, a serious subject.[3] Christ has loved mankind more than the angels that fell.[4] The loadstone, despising the gold and pearl, draws the iron to it: thus Christ passed by the angels, who were of a more noble extract, and drew mankind to him. Christ loved us more than his own life; nay, though we had a hand in his death, yet that he should not leave us out of his will, this is a love "which passeth knowledge."[5] Who can read this without seriousness? The Scripture speaks of the mystery of faith, the eter-nal recompenses, the paucity of them that shall be saved: "Few chosen."[6] One says,[7] the names of all the

---

1 "It is not an empty word, that it should be despised by you."—PAGNINO. *(Nichols' trans.)*

2 Deuteronomy 32:47.

3 Titus 3:4.

4 Hebrews 2:16.

5 Ephesians 3:19.

6 Matthew 20:16.

7 FLAVIUS VOPISCUS.

good emperors of Rome might be engraven in a little ring. There are but a few names in the book of life. The Scripture speaks of "striving" for heaven as in an agony;[1,2] it cautions us of falling short of the "promised rest;"[3] it describes the horror of the infernal torments, "the worm and the fire."[4,5] Who can read this, and not be serious? Some have light, feathery spirits; they run over the most weighty truths in haste; like Israel, who ate the Passover in haste; and they are not benefited by the Word. Read with a solemn, composed spirit. Seriousness is the Christian's ballast, which keeps him from being overturned with vanity.

DIRECTION 7. *Labor to remember what you read.*—Satan would steal the Word out of our mind;[6] not that he intends to make use of it himself, but lest we should make use of it. The memory should be like the chest in the ark, where the law was put. "I have remembered thy judgments of old."[7,8] Jerome writes of that religious lady Paula, that she had got most of the Scriptures by heart. We are bid to have

---

1 "We must wrestle as for life or death."—CORNELIUS A LAPIDE. *(Nichols' trans.)*

2 Luke 13:24.

3 Hebrews 4:1.

4 "The damned in hell will so die as to be always alive, and will so live as to be always dying."—BERNARD. *(Nichols' trans.)*

5 Mark 9:44.

6 Matthew 13:4, 19.

7 Psalm 119:52.

8 "Memory is an inward scribe or recorder."—NICHOLS.

the "Word dwell in" us.[1,2] The Word is a jewel that adorns the hidden man; and shall we not remember it? "Can a maid forget her ornaments?"[3] Such as have a disease they call *lienteria*, [in which] the meat comes up as fast as they eat it, and stays not in the stomach, are not nourished by it. If the Word stays not in the memory, it cannot profit. Some can better remember a piece of news than a line of Scripture; their memories are like those ponds, where the frogs live, but the fish die.

DIRECTION 8. *Meditate upon what you read.*— "I will meditate in thy precepts."[4] The Hebrew word הָגָה "to meditate," signifies, "to be intense in the mind."[5] In meditation there must be a fixing of the thoughts upon the object: the Virgin Mary "pondered" those things, etc.[6] Meditation is the concoction of Scripture: reading brings a truth into our head, meditation brings it into our heart: reading and meditation must, like Castor and Pollux, appear together. Meditation without reading is erroneous; reading without meditation is barren. The bee sucks the flower, then works it in the hive, and

---

1 "'Let it dwell in you,' that is, let it not fall from your memory."—NICHOLS.
2 Colossians 3:16.
3 Jeremiah 2:32.
4 Psalm 119:15.
5 "We should use much reflection."—CHRYSOSTOM. *(Nichols' trans.)*
6 Luke 2:19.

so turns it to honey: by reading we suck the flower of the Word, by meditation we work it in the hive of our mind, and so it turns to profit. Meditation is the bellows of the affections: "While I was musing the fire burned."[1] The reason we come away so cold from reading the Word is, because we do not warm ourselves at the fire of meditation.

DIRECTION 9. *Come to the reading of Scripture with humble hearts.*—Acknowledge how unworthy you are that God should reveal himself in his Word to you. God's secrets are with the humble: pride is an enemy to profiting. It is observed [that] the ground on which the peacock sits is barren: that heart where pride sits is barren. An arrogant person disdains the counsels of the Word, and hates the reproofs; is he likely to profit "God giveth grace unto the humble."[2] The eminentest saints have been but of low stature in their own eyes; like the sun in the zenith, they showed least when they were at the highest. David had "more understanding than all his teachers."[3] But how humble was he! "I am a worm, and no man."[4] *David* in the Arabic tongue signifies a "worm."[5]

DIRECTION 10. *Give credence to the Word*

---

1 Psalm 39:3.
2 James 4:6.
3 Psalm 119:99.
4 Psalm 22:6.
5 "Generous and noble in his conduct, but humble in his own estimation."—GREGORY OF NAZIANZUS. *(Nichols' trans.)*

written.—Believe it to be of God; see the name of God in every line. The Romans, that they might gain credit to their laws, reported that they were inspired by the gods at Rome. Believe the Scripture to be *coelo missa* "divinely inspired." "All Scripture is," θεόπνευστος "of divine inspiration."[1] Who but God could reveal the great doctrines of the Trinity, the hypostatical union, the resurrection? Whence should the Scripture come, if not from God? 1. *Sinners* could not be the authors of Scripture. Would they indite such holy lines? or inveigh so fiercely against those sins which they love? 2. *Saints* could not be the authors of Scripture. How could it stand with their sanctity to counterfeit God's name, and put "Thus saith the Lord" to a book of their own devising? 3. *Angels* could not be the authors of Scripture. What angel in heaven dare personate God, and say, "I am the Lord?" Believe the pedigree of Scripture to be sacred, and to come from the "Father of lights."[2] The Scripture's antiquity speaks its divinity. No human histories extant reach further than Noah's flood; but the Scripture writes of things before time.[3] Besides, the majesty, profundity, purity, harmony, of Scripture show it could be breathed from none but God himself. Add to this the

---

1 2 Timothy 3:16.

2 James 1:17.

3 "That is true, which is first in order of time." —Tertullian. (*Nichols' trans.*)

efficacy the Word written has had upon men's consciences.[1] By reading Scripture they have been turned into other men; as might be instanced in St. Austin, Junius, and others. If you should set a seal upon a piece of marble, and it should leave a print behind, you would say there was a strange virtue in that seal: so, that the Word written should leave a heavenly print of grace upon the heart, it argues it to be of divine authority. If you would profit by the Word, believe it to be of God. Some sceptics question the verity of Scripture; though they have the articles of religion in their "creed," yet not in their *belief.* "Who hath believed our report?"[2] Unbelief enervates the virtue of the Word, and makes it abortive: who will obey those truths he does not believe?[3] "The Word did not profit them, not being mixed with faith."[4]

DIRECTION 11. *Highly prize the Scriptures.*— "The law of thy mouth is better to me than thousands of gold and silver."[5] Can *he* make a proficiency in any art, *who* slights and deprecate it? Prize this book of God above all other books. St. Gregory calls the Bible "the heart and soul of God." The rabbins say, that there is a mountain of sense hangs

1 "When the Scripture comes in contact with the mind, it acts like lightning."—LUTHER. *(Nichols' trans.)*
2 Isaiah 53:1.
3 "Where the belief is wrong and defective, there the conduct will be immoral."—HIERONYMUS. *(Nichols' trans.)*
4 Hebrews 4:2.
5 Psalm 119:72.

upon every *apex* and tittle of Scripture. "The law of the Lord is perfect."[1,2] The Scripture is the library of the Holy Ghost; it is a pandect of divine knowledge, an exact model and platform of religion.[3] The Scripture contains in it the *credenda*, "the things which we are to believe," and the *agenda*, "the things which we are to practice." It is "able to make us wise unto salvation."[4] "The Scripture is the standard of truth," the judge of controversies;[5] it is the pole-star to direct us to heaven.[6,7] "The commandment is a lamp."[8,9] The Scripture is the compass by which the rudder of our will is to be steered; it is the field in which Christ, the Pearl of price, is hid; it is a rock of diamonds; it is a sacred *collyrium*, or "eye-salve;" it mends *their* eyes *that* look upon it; it is a spiritual optic-glass in which the glory of God is resplendent; it is the panacy or "universal medicine" for the soul.[10] The leaves of Scripture are

---

1 Psalm 19:7.

2 "It contains all things necessary to perfect piety."
—MUSCULUS, CAMERO. *(Nichols' trans.)*

3 "I adore the fullness and completeness of Scripture."
—TERTULLIAN. *(Nichols' trans.)*

4 2 Timothy 3:15.

5 RIVITUS, IRENAEUS.

6 Isaiah 8:20.

7 QUISTORPIUS.

8 Proverbs 6:23.

9 "It is a light which is common to every man, and enlightens all."—CLEMENT OF ALEXANDRIA. *(Nichols' trans.)*

10 QUISTORPIUS.

like the "leaves of the tree of life, for the healing of the nations."[1] The Scripture is both the breeder and feeder of grace.[2] How is the convert born, but by "the word of truth?"[3] How does he grow, but by "the sincere milk of the Word?"[4] The Word written is the book out of which our evidences for heaven are fetched; it is the sea-mark which shows us the rocks of sin to avoid; it is the antidote against error and apostasy, the two-edged sword which wounds the old serpent. It is our bulwark to withstand the force of lust; like the Capitol of Rome, which was a place of strength and ammunition. The Scripture is the "tower of David," whereon the shields of our faith hang.[5] "Take away the Word, and you deprive us of the sun," said Luther. The Word written is above an angelic embassy, or voice from heaven. "This voice which came from heaven we heard." We have also, βεϐαιοτρον λογον "a more sure word."[6] O, prize the Word written; prizing is the way to profiting. If Caesar so valued his Commentaries, that for preserving them he lost his purple robe, how should we estimate the sacred oracles of God? "I have esteemed the words of his mouth more than my necessary

---

1 Revelation 22:2.
2 "The nourishment of life."—ATHANASIUS. *(Nichols' trans.)*
3 James 1:18.
4 1 Peter 2:2.
5 Song of Solomon 4:4.
6 2 Peter 1:18, 19.

food."[1] King Edward the Sixth, on the day of his coronation, had presented before him three swords, signifying that he was monarch of three kingdoms. The king said, there was one sword wanting: being asked what that was, [he] answered, "The Holy Bible, which is the sword of the Spirit, and is to be preferred before these ensigns of royalty." Robert king of Sicily did so prize God's Word, that, speaking to his friend Petrarcha, he said, "I protest, the Scriptures are dearer to me than my kingdom; and if I must be deprived of one of them, I had rather lose my diadem than the Scriptures."[2]

DIRECTION 12. *Get an ardent love to the Word.*—Prizing relates to the judgment, love to the affections. "Consider how I love thy precepts."[3] He is likely to grow rich who delights in his trade; he who is φιλομαθης will be ϖολυμαθης "a lover of learning will be a scholar." St. Austin tells us, before his conversion he took no pleasure in the Scriptures, but afterwards they were his "chaste delights."[4] David tasted the Word "sweeter than the honey which drops from the comb."[5] Psalm 19:10. Thomas a Kempis

---

1 Job 23:12.
2 CORNELIUS A LAPIDE.
3 Psalm 119:159; Romans 7:22.
4 AUGUSTINE.
5 "That which drops freely from the honeycomb, is called 'the cream or marrow of the honey;' but more delicious draughts of honied sweetness are imbibed from the breasts of Holy Scripture."—NICHOLS.

used to say, he found no content but to be *in angulo cum libello* "in a corner, with the book of God in his hand." Did Alphonsus king of Sicily recover of a fit of sickness with that great pleasure he took in reading of Quintus Curtius? What infinite pleasure should we take in reading the book of life! There is enough in the Word to breed holy complacency and delight; it is a specimen and demonstration of God's love to us. The Spirit is God's love-token, the Word his love-letter. How does one delight to read over his friend's letter! The Word written is a divine treasury, or storehouse;[1] in it are scattered truths as pearls, to adorn "the hidden man of the heart." The Word written is the true manna, which has all sorts of sweet taste in it; in it is a sovereign elixir, it "gives wine to them of an heavy heart." I have read of an ancient rabbi, who in a great concourse of people made proclamation of a sovereign cordial he had to sell: many resorting to him, and asking him to show it, he opened the Bible, and directed them to several places of comfort in it. Holy David drank of this cordial. "This is my comfort in my affliction: for thy Word has quickened me."[2] Γλυκεια και αληθεια ["It combines sweetness with truth."] St. Chrysostom compares the Scripture to a garden;[3] every line in it is a

1 QUISTORPIUS.
2 Psalm 119:50.
3 "A pleasure-garden is sweet; but much sweeter is the perusal of the sacred writings. The former contains fading flowers; but the latter blooming thoughts. There the cooling zephyr

fragrant flower, which we should wear, not in our bosom, but our heart. Delight in the Word causes profit: and we must not only love the comforts of the Word, but the reproofs. Myrrh is bitter to the palate, but good for the stomach.

DIRECTION 13. *Come to the reading of the Word with honest hearts.*—Christ speaks of the καρδια καλη "the honest heart."[1]

QUESTION. "What is it to read the Word with an honest heart?"

ANSWER 1. *To come with an heart willing to know the whole counsel of God.*—A good heart would not have any truth concealed; but says, as Job, "That which I see not, teach thou me."[2] When men pick and choose in religion, they will do some things the Word enjoins them, but not others. These are unsound hearts, and are not benefited by holy writ. These are like a patient, who having a bitter pill prescribed, and a julep, he will take the julep, but refuses the pill.

2. To read the Word with an honest heart, is *to read it that we may be made better by it.*[3]—The Word is, *quoad se*, the medium and organ of sanctity; and we come to it not only to illuminate us, but

plays; but here we are refreshed by the breath of the Holy Spirit."—CHRYSOSTOM *Homil. in Psalm 44. (Nichols' trans.)*

1 Luke 8:15.

2 Job 34:32.

3 "'An honest heart,' that is, one whose intense desire is to advance in the divine life."—BRUGENSIS. *(Nichols' trans.)*

consecrate us: "Sanctify them through thy truth."[1]
Some go to the Bible, as one goes to the garden, to
pick flowers, that is, fine notions. Austin confesses,
that before his conversion he went to hear Ambrose
more for the elegancy of speech and quaintness of
notion, than the spirituality of the matter. This is like
a woman that paints her face, but neglects her health.
But *this* is to have an honest heart, when we come to
the Scriptures as Naaman to the waters of Jordan, to
be healed of our leprosy. "O," says the soul, "that this
sword of the Spirit may pierce the rock of my heart;
that this blessed Word may have such a virtue in it, as
the water of jealousy, to kill and make fruitful;[2] that
it may kill my sin, and make me fruitful in grace."

DIRECTION 14. *Learn to apply Scripture.*—
Take every word as spoken to yourselves. When the
Word thunders against sin, think thus: "God means
my sins;" when it presses any duty, "God intends me
in this." Many put off Scripture from themselves,
as if it only concerned those who lived in the time
when it was written; but if you intend to profit by
the Word, bring it home to yourselves: a medicine
will do no good, unless it be applied. The saints of
old took the Word as if it had been spoken to them
by name. When king Josiah heard the threatening
which was written in the book of God, he applied it
to himself: "He rent his clothes, and humbled" his

---

1 John 17:17.
2 Numbers 5:27, 28.

soul "before the Lord."[1]

DIRECTION 15. *Observe the preceptive part of the Word, as well as the promissive.*[2]—The precepts carry duty in them, like the veins which carry the blood; the promises carry comfort in them, like the arteries which carry the spirits. Make use as well of the precepts to direct you, as the promises to comfort you. Such as cast their eye upon the promise, with a neglect of the command, are not edified by Scripture; they look more after comfort than duty. They mistake their comforts, as Apollo embraced the laurel-tree instead of Daphne. The body may be swelled with wind as well as flesh: a man may be filled with false comfort, as well as that which is genuine and real.

DIRECTION 16. *Let your thoughts dwell upon the most material passages of Scripture.*—The bee fastens on those flowers where she may suck most sweetness. Though the whole contexture of Scripture is excellent, yet some parts of it may have a greater emphasis, and be more quick and pungent. Reading the names of the tribes, or the genealogies of the patriarchs, is not of the same importance as faith and "the new creature." Mind the *magnalia legis*, the "weighty things of the law."[3] They who read only to satisfy their curiosity, do rather busy than profit

---

1 2 Kings 22:11, 13.
2 Promissive—making a promise; implying a promise; promising.—*Webster's 1913 Dictionary.*
3 Hosea 8:12.

themselves. The searching too far into Christ's temporal reign has, I fear, weakened his spiritual reign in some men's hearts.

DIRECTION 17. *Compare yourselves with the Word.*—See how the Scripture and your hearts agree, how your dial goes with this sun. Are your hearts, as it were, a transcript and counterpane[1] of Scripture? Is the Word copied out into your hearts? The Word calls for humility; are you not only humbled, but humble? The Word calls for regeneration;[2] have you the signature and engraving of the Holy Ghost upon you? have you a change of heart? not only a partial and moral change, but a spiritual? Is there such a change wrought in you, as if another soul did live in the same body? "Such were some of you; but ye are washed, but ye are sanctified," etc.[3,4] The Word calls for love to the saints;[5] do you love grace where you see it?[6] Do you love grace in a poor man as well as in a rich?

---

1 One of two deeds, or the true copy of a deed or other legal instrument; a term now superseded by the word *counterpart.* —NICHOLS.

2 John 3:7.

3 1 Corinthians 6:11.

4 "Similar expressions are employed by Gregory Nazianzen, in his funeral oration in praise of Cyprian, where he relates his wonderful 'change or transition' after divine grace had visited his heart."—NICHOLS.

5 1 Peter 1:22.

6 "There is the same drawing of the mind towards the similitude of an object, as towards the object itself."—NICHOLS.

A son loves to see his father's picture, though hung in a mean frame; do you love grace, though mixed with some failings, as we love gold, though it be in the ore? The bringing the rule of the Word and our hearts together, to see how they agree, would prove very advantageous to us. Hereby we come to know the true complexion and state of our souls, and see what evidences and certificates we have for heaven.

DIRECTION 18. *Take special notice of those Scriptures which speak to your particular case.*— Were a consumptive person to read Galen or Hippocrates, he would chiefly observe what they wrote about a consumption. Great regard is to be had to those paragraphs of Scripture, which are most apposite to one's present case. I shall instance only in three cases: 1. Affliction. 2. Desertion. 3. Sin.

CASE I. First, *Affliction.*—*Has God made your chain heavy?* Consult these Scriptures:[1] "If ye endure chastening, God dealeth with you as sons." "By this shall the iniquity of Jacob be purged; and this is all the fruit to take away his sin."[2, 3] "Your sorrow shall

---

1 Hebrews 12:7. See Job 36:8, 9; Deuteronomy 8:15; 1 Kings 11:39; Psalm 89:30–33; Hebrews 12:10, 11; Psalm 37:39; Romans 8:28; 1 Peter 1:6, 7; 2 Chronicles 33:11–13; Revelation 3:19; 2 Corinthians 4:16; Job 5:17; Micah 6:9.

2 "While the lustful flesh is thus bruised by the scourgings of God, the mind towers to the skies on the powerful wings of the virtues."—BERNARD, Serm. 10. *De Dominicâ Coenâ. (Nichols' trans.)*

3 Isaiah 27:9.

be turned into joy."[1] The French have a berry, which they call *uve de spine*, "the grape of a thorn." God gives joy out of sorrow; here is the grape of a thorn: "Our light affliction, which is but for a moment, worketh for us a far more exceeding and eternal weight of glory."[2] The limner lays his gold upon dark colors: God first lays the dark color of affliction, and then the golden color of glory.

CASE II. Secondly, *Desertion.—Are your spiritual comforts eclipsed?*[3] "In a little wrath I hid my face from thee for a moment: but with everlasting kindness will I have mercy on thee." The sun may hide itself in a cloud, but it is not out of the firmament; God may hide his face, but he is not out of covenant. "I will not be always wroth: for the spirit should fail before me, and the souls which I have made."[4] God is like the musician, he will not stretch the strings of his lute too hard, lest they break. "Light is sown for the righteous."[5] A saint's comfort may be hid as seed under the clods, but at last it will spring up into an harvest of joy.

CASE III. Thirdly, *Sin.—1. Are you drawn away with lust?* Read Galatians 5:24; James 1:15; 1 Peter

1 John 16:20.
2 2 Corinthians 4:17.
3 Isaiah 54:8. See also Lamentations 3:31–33; Psalm 106:6, 9; 103:9; Mark 15:34; Isaiah 8:17; 49:15; 50:10; 54:10; 2 Corinthians 7:6.
4 Isaiah 57:16.
5 Psalm 97:11.

2:11. "Abstain from fleshly lusts, which war against the soul."[1] Lust kills with embracing. "There met him a woman with the attire of an harlot. He goeth after her straightway, as an ox goeth to the slaughter; till a dart strike through his liver," etc.[2,3] "The mouth of strange women is a deep pit: he that is abhorred of the Lord shall fall therein."[4] Go to the waters of the sanctuary to quench the fire of lust.

2. *Are you under the power of unbelief?*—Read Isaiah 26:3: "Thou wilt keep him in perfect peace," שָׁלוֹם שָׁלוֹם ; ["peace, peace,"] "whose mind is stayed on thee: because he trusteth in thee." Mr. Bolton speaks of a distressed soul who found much comfort from this Scripture on his sick bed: "The Word of the Lord is tried: he is a buckler to all them that trust in him."[5] "That whosoever believeth in him should not perish."[6] Unbelief is a God affronting sin: "He that believeth not God, hath made him a liar."[7] It is a soul-murdering sin: "He that believeth not the Son shall not see life; but the wrath of God

---

1 "Lawless desires are the gates of hell, through which men descend to the infernal regions."—NICHOLS.
2 Proverbs 7:10, 22, 23.
3 "Plato makes the liver the seat of lust or eager desire." —NICHOLS.
4 Proverbs 22:14.
5 2 Samuel 22:31. See also Zephaniah 3:12; Psalm 34:22; 55:22; 32:10; Mark 9:23; 1 Peter 5:7.
6 John 3:15.
7 1 John 5:10.

abideth on him."[1] Thus, in reading observe those Scriptures which do *rem acu tangere*, "touch upon your particular case." Although all the Bible must be read; yet those texts which point most directly to your condition, be sure to put a special star upon.

DIRECTION 19. *Take special notice of the examples in Scripture.*—Make the examples of others living sermons to you.[2]

1. *Observe the examples of God's judgments upon sinners.*—They have been hanged up in chains *in terrorem.* How severely has God punished proud men! Nebuchadnezzar was turned to grass, Herod eaten up with vermin. How has God plagued idolaters![3] What a swift witness has he been against liars![4] These examples are set-up as sea-marks to avoid.[5]

2. *Observe the examples of God's mercy to saints.*—Jeremy was preserved in the dungeon, the three children in the furnace, Daniel in the lions' den. These examples are props to faith, spurs to holiness.

DIRECTION 20. *Leave not off reading in the Bible till you find your hearts warmed.* —"I will never forget thy precepts: for with them thou hast quickened me."[6] Read the Word, not only as a history, but labor

---

1 John 3:36.
2 "Precepts teach us that which is right; but examples are motives for us to practice it."—NICHOLS.
3 Numbers 25:3–5, 9; 1 Kings 14:9–11.
4 Acts 5:5, 10.
5 1 Corinthians 10:11; Jude 7.
6 Psalm 119:93.

to be affected with it. Let it not only inform you, but inflame you. "Is not my Word like as a fire? saith the Lord."[1] Go not from the Word till you can say as those disciples, "Did not our heart burn within us?"[2]

DIRECTION 21. *Set upon the practice of what you read.*—"I have done thy commandments."[3,4] A student in physic does not satisfy himself to read over a system or body of physic, but he falls upon practicing physic: the life-blood of religion lies in the practic part. So, in the text: "He shall read" in the book of the law "all the days of his life: that he may learn to keep all the words of this law and these statutes, to do them."[5] Christians should be walking Bibles. Xenophon said, "Many read Lycurgus's laws, but few observe them." The Word written is not only a rule of knowledge, but a rule of obedience:[6] it is not only to mend our sight, but to mend our pace. David calls God's Word "a lamp unto his feet."[7] It was not only a light to his eyes to see by,

1 Jeremiah 23:29.
2 Luke 24:32.
3 "The beauty of the soul springs from obedience."
—CHRYSOSTOM. *(Nichols' trans.)*
4 Psalm 119:166.
5 "We can be said to know only so much as we practice."
—NICHOLS.
6 "He is mindful of the law in a two-fold manner *who* does not forget to perform its commands."—BILLII *Anthologia. (Nichols' trans.)*
7 Psalm 119:105.

but to his feet to walk by. By practice we trade the talent of knowledge, and turn it to profit. This is a blessed reading of Scripture, when we fly from the sins which the Word forbids, and espouse the duties which the Word commands. Reading without practice will be but a torch to light men to hell.

DIRECTION 22. *Make use of Christ's prophetical office.*—He is "the Lion of the tribe of Judah," to whom it is given "to open the book" of God, "and to loose the seven seals thereof."[1,2] Christ does so teach as he quickens. "I am the light of the world: he that followeth me shall have," *lumen vitae,* "the light of life."[3] The philosopher says, "Light and heat increase together." It is true here: where Christ comes into the soul with his light, there is the heat of spiritual life going along with it. Christ gives us *spiritualem gustum,* "a taste of the Word:" "Thou hast taught me. How sweet are thy words unto my taste!"[4] It is one thing to read a promise, another thing to "taste" it. Such as would be Scripture-proficients, let them get Christ to be their teacher. "Then opened he their understanding, that they might understand the Scriptures."[5] Christ did

---

1 "The revealer of the secret things of God."—PAREUS. *(Nichols' trans.)*
2 Revelation 5:5.
3 John 8:12.
4 Psalm 119:102, 103.
5 Luke 24:45.

not only open the Scriptures, but "opened their understanding."[1]

DIRECTION 23. *Tread often upon the threshold of the sanctuary.*—Wait diligently on a rightly constituted ministry: "Blessed is the man that heareth me, watching diligently at my gates, waiting at the posts of my doors."[2] Ministers are God's interpreters; it is their work to expound and open dark places of Scripture. We read of "pitchers, and lamps within the pitchers."[3] Ministers are "earthen" pitchers.[4] But these pitchers have lamps within them, to light souls in the dark.

DIRECTION 24. *Pray that God will make you profit.*—"I am the Lord thy God, which teacheth thee to profit."[5] Make David's prayer: "Open thou mine eyes, that I may behold wondrous things out of thy law."[6] Pray to God to take off the veil on the Scripture, that you may understand it; and the veil on your heart, that you may believe it. Pray that God will not only give you his Word as a *rule* of holiness, but his grace as a *principle* of holiness. Implore the guidance of God's Spirit: "Thou gavest

---

1 "He has his throne in heaven, who instructs the hearts of the faithful on earth."—AUGUSTINE. *(Nichols' trans.)*
2 Proverbs 8:34.
3 Judges 7:16.
4 2 Corinthians 4:7.
5 Isaiah 48:17.
6 Psalm 119:18.

them thy good Spirit to instruct them."[1,2] Though the ship has compass to sail by, and store of tackling, yet without a gale of wind it cannot sail. Though we have the Word written as our compass to sail by, and make use of our endeavors as the tackling, yet, unless the Spirit of God blow upon us, we cannot sail with profit. When the Almighty is as "dew" unto us, then we "grow as the lily," and our "beauty is as the olive-tree."[3] Beg the anointing of the Holy Ghost.[4] One may see the figures on a dial, but he cannot tell how the day goes unless the sun shine: we may read many truths in the Bible, but we cannot know them savingly till God's Spirit shine in our souls.[5] The Spirit is, "a Spirit of wisdom and revelation."[6,7] When Philip joined himself to the eunuch's chariot, then he understood Scripture.[8] When God's Spirit joins himself to the Word, then it will be effectual to salvation.

These rules observed, the Word written would,

---

1 "Christ, sitting at the right hand of God, has sent in his stead the power of the Holy Ghost."—TERTULLIAN. *(Nichols' trans.)*

2 Nehemiah 9:20.

3 Hosea 14:5, 6.

4 1 John 2:20.

5 2 Corinthians 4:6.

6 Ephesians 1:17.

7 "Πνευμα σοφιας και αποκαλυψεως."

8 Acts 8:29–35.

through God's blessing, be "an engrafted word."[1,2] A good scion[3] grafted into a bad stock changes the nature of it, and makes it bear sweet and generous fruit; so when the Word is grafted savingly into men's hearts, it sanctifies them, and make them bring forth the sweet "fruits of righteousness."[4]

Thus I have answered this question, *How we may read the Scriptures with most spiritual profit.*

I shall conclude all with two corollaries:

1. *Content not yourselves with the bare reading of Scripture, but labor to find some spiritual increment and profit.*—Get the Word transcribed into your hearts: "The law of his God is in his heart."[5] Never leave till you are assimilated into the Word. Such as profit by reading of the book of God are the best Christians alive; they answer God's cost, they credit religion, they save their souls.

2. *You who have profited by reading the Holy Scriptures, adore God's distinguishing grace.*— Bless God that he has not only brought the light to you, but opened your eyes to see it; that he has unlocked his hid treasure, and enriched you with saving knowledge. Some perish by *not having* Scripture, and others by *not improving* it. That

1 James 1:21.
2 "εμφυτος λογος."
3 Scion—a shoot or sprout of a plant; a sucker. *(Webster's 1913 Dictionary)*
4 Philippians 1:11.
5 Psalm 37:31.

God should pass by millions in the world, and the lot of his electing love should fall upon you; that the Scripture, like the pillar of cloud, should have a dark side to others, but a light side to you; that to others it should be a "dead letter," but to you the "savor of life;" that Christ should not only be revealed *to* you, but *in* you;[1] how should you be in an holy ecstasy of wonder, and wish that you had hearts of seraphim burning in love to God, and the voices of angels, to make heaven ring with God's praises!

OBJECTION. But some of the godly may say, they fear they do not profit by the Word they read.

RESPONSE. As in the body, when there is a lipothymy or "fainting of the vital spirits," cordials are applied: so let me apply a few divine cordials to such as are ready to faint under the fear of non-proficiency.

1. *You may profit by reading the Word, though you come short of others.*—The ground which brought forth but thirty-fold was "good ground."[2] Say not you are non-proficients, because you do not go in equipage with other eminent saints: those were counted strong men among David's worthies, though they did not attain to the honor of the first three.[3]

2. *You may profit by reading the Word, though*

---

1 Galatians 1:16.
2 Matthew 13:8.
3 2 Samuel 23:19, 22, 23.

you are not of so quick apprehension.—Some impeach themselves of non-proficiency, because they are but slow of understanding. When our blessed Saviour foretold his sufferings, the apostles themselves "understood not, and it was hid from them."[1] The author to the Hebrews speaks of some who were *segnes auribus,* "dull of hearing;"[2] yet they belonged to the election. Such as have weaker judgments may have stronger affections. Leah was tender-eyed, yet fruitful. A Christian's intellectuals may be less quick and penetrating, yet that little knowledge he has of Scripture keeps him from sin; as a man that has but weak sight, yet it keeps him from falling into the water.

3. *You may profit by reading Scripture, though you have not so excellent memories.*—Many complain their memories leak.

Nec retinent patulae commissa fideliter aures.[3]
—HORATII *Epist.* lib. i. ep. xviii. 70.

Christian, are you grieved you can remember no more? Then, for your comfort,

(1.) *You may have a good heart, though you have not so good a memory.*

(2.) *Though you can not remember all you read,*

---

1 Luke 9:45.
2 Hebrews 5:11.
3 "Their leaky ears no secret can retain."—*(Duncombe's Trans.)*

yet you remember that which is most material, and which you have most need of.—At a feast we do not eat of every dish, but we take so much as nourishes. It is with a good Christian's memory as it is with a lamp: though the lamp be not full of oil, yet it has so much oil as makes the lamp burn: though your memory be not full of Scripture, yet you retain so much as makes your love to God burn. Then be of good comfort; you profit by what you read; and take notice of that encouraging Scripture: "The Comforter, which is the Holy Ghost, he shall bring all things to your remembrance."[1]

---

1 John 14:26.

www.ingramcontent.com/pod-product-compliance
Lightning Source LLC
Chambersburg PA
CBHW020440030426
42337CB00014B/1334